CHIVALRY
IS NOT DEAD

BY

ANTHONY RAY WILLIAMS

Tate Publishing, LLC.

"Chivalry is Not Dead" by Anthony Ray Williams

Published in the United States of America
by Tate Publishing, LLC
127 East Trade Center Terrace
Mustang, OK 73064
(888) 361–9473

ISBN: 1-5988618-5-9

ACKNOWLEDGMENTS

I cannot fully express my gratitude to the exceptional team at Tate Publishing, for their generosity, faith, and superb guidance. Thanks especially to Dr. Richard Tate, who believed in me and this book from the start. My thanks also to the initial core of early supporters, Kimberly Spears, Marie-Fleur and Eloise, Lisa Carroll, Marilyn Calabrese, Olivia Holt, and all the talented people at Agape International Spiritual Center.

And finally, I would be remiss if I did not mention the extraordinary women and men who have touched my life. First, my mother, Annie - nurturer, friend, and role model. Thanks for providing the foundation for my own path to happiness in life. My father, Nelson E Harmon Sr.: thanks for being there in your own special way. And thanks to my siblings, Mary, Sandy, Lonnie and Nelson Jr., and my nieces and nephews too many to name.

Table of Contents

INTRODUCTION

Chivalry is Not Dead offers a model for men of the 21st Century. It teaches that treating people with respect, gives them responsibility, and holds them strictly accountable because it's the honorable thing to do, not just because it makes good sense. More than any book you've ever read on the subject, *Chivalry is Not Dead* will compel men to question everything they know about relationships.

Can you imagine a world where people display chivalry, love, honor, and respect? A world where gentlemen act like gentlemen and ladies like ladies.

Today, chivalry is a concept that is largely ignored. It is something that is known to literary scholars and history professors, but it doesn't seem to have any place in the world of business, politics, relationships or personal conduct in the modern world. Women have been taught that displays of chivalry is demeaning and condescending, and men have come to believe that courtesy and respectful attitudes aren't "manly" disposition.

Current events and front-page headlines have made us all aware of the importance of ethical conduct and personal integrity. In the wake of scandals and betrayals of public trust, people are recognizing that duty, heroism, honesty and self-respect are more valuable today than ever before.

People should realize that the 21st Century needs a Code of Chivalry. I challenge men to consider how the Code of Chivalry can be put to use in their lives each day. I wrote this book to demonstrate that chivalry can help us instill values in our children and our own lives, which it can change the way we manage our relationships with others and conduct business; that it can help establish goals and overcome challenges.

Perhaps my stand is the struggle to break the stronghold of men's values today and replace it with more timeless values: integrity, fairness, social responsibility, and above all respect towards women.

There will be grave differences of opinion on what duties and actions are expected in service of these virtues, and of their relative importance to one another, but I hope this serves as starting point of discussion.

I

CHIVALRY IS NOT DEAD!

At one point in my life, I really thought I had it all figured out. I was working in what I thought was my dream job, making a decent living, and was buying my first home. Then, one day I woke up depressed. During the night, when I was asleep, I came to a decision to tell myself the truth. I disliked my job and the 2 hour drive I had to make every morning. I was lonely living in my new home and city where I knew no one and I had just broken up with my girlfriend of six years. People looking from the outside thought I had really made it! Who was I to doubt them?

Although I did not realize it at the time, I was lucky. There was one person in my life that immediately recognized my confusion, anger, and loneliness. This very astute individual went so far as to detect an even greater vulnerability. It was a fear that my life was going to end, and I would have nothing to show for it. For some reason I was not willing to recognize this fear. Most importantly, this person recognized that beneath it all there was a need for me to grow, a need for me to change. I needed structure–a foundation to change the way I treated and honored women.

Growing up in a home with four siblings, I being the middle child, both parents had to work. They provided us with a home, food on the table and a bed to sleep in. I had nothing really to complain about, other than my big brother kept wearing my clothes. As I got older and left my home of security, I found myself without some fundamentals of life. Sure, mom and dad had taught me how to cook, clean and basically how to treat people with respect. What I didn't know was how to truly relate to women. I found myself consistently at odds with having appreciation for woman. This confusion went way into my late 30s. After years of unsuccessful relationships, I came to realize the truth was there was no text book to follow, no man to look up to, and no idea about what it was to be a man or any idea about chivalry. It was then I started to understand that I had not been given the basic tools for a relationships or commitment. Sure, I had some understanding on how to relate to women, have an intelligent conversation, and treat women with respect. But what I didn't know was how to be a real man. I had no loyalty or commitment, nor did I know what my responsibilities were or how to treat the woman in my life.

During my youth, I would watch movies with Ginger Rogers and Fred Astair dancing. During that time, I never once asked myself, who is leading whom. It was exciting just watching poetry in motion. It didn't matter who was leading or who followed. They did it together. I would watch movies where men act like gentlemen; they would take their coats off if a woman was cold, hold open the door so she could walk though, and tip their hats at the same time. They made sure the woman walked on the inside away from the streets just in case a car would come by and splash water. They would stand when a woman entered the room and look her in the eyes while having a conversation. Sure, this was just a movie, but life has been known to imitate art. Our actions are influenced everyday by what we see on TV, watch at the movies and hear on the radio. So why can't we imitate art that is of honor, loyalty, duty, and chivalry?

In writing this book, it is my hope to offer support and guidance to those who are looking for structure and a foundation in the way they treat women. Those who are wise enough or courageous enough to pick up this book will be equipped to meet the tasks that lie ahead. No matter which category you fall in, I want to share with you the things I found to be most effective in helping me to remain open and grounded in the knowledge of who I really am when life experiences threaten to make me forget. The moment you realize that the ways you are thinking and feeling and treating a woman do not work for you, the information in this book will be something new for you to try. If you have received this book as a gift and don't know why, take a hint!

Does chivalry have a place in the modern world? The ideal of chivalry still exist and is being integrated into life as we know it today. Not only is there a Broadway musical entitled Camelot but the morals and beliefs of chivalry still thrive in the present day world. Chivalry defined the relationships between women and men. The men strive to attain their lady's affections by romancing them. Men were to devote themselves entirely to one woman. This can still be true today.

WHERE DOES CHIVALRY STEM FROM, HOW DID IT BEGIN?

Chiv-al-ry\shiv-el-re\: A body of knights, the system, spirit, ways, or customs of knighthood.

1. Qualities of ideal knight: the combination of qualities expected of the ideal medieval knight, especially courage, honor, loyalty, and consideration for others, *especially woman.*
   Encarta ® World English Dictionary © & (P) 1998– 2004 Microsoft Corporation. All rights reserved.

During the 12th Century, as society began to really settle, two important things happened to the ideals of what was first called "knighthood." First, the church began to reshape the idea of the social warrior to its own ends. Knights were called to crusade, to be the "Soldiers of GOD." The crusades were launched. The ideal put forward by the church sought to add new virtues to the potent strength of the warrior. The idea was that with GOD and right on one side, the knight was strengthened. The church added Godliness, justice, defense of the innocent and the weak, honesty, humility and decency.

Along with the rise of the new "religious" chivalry, secular influences arose that had an equally strong say in the new reality of knighthood. The idea was of Courtly Love, a new cult of love. The central occupant in this school of thought was that through love, the knight or lover could be strengthened by the love of a woman. This was completely different from the ideals of the religious chivalry, where the knight was strengthened by devotion to GOD. From the courts of love, chivalry acquired courtesy, generosity, loyalty, and the respect and defense of *all women.*

Chivalric virtues were a crystal clear refinement of what it meant to be a fine human being, a person in search of justice, humility and love. These standards grew and changed over time, until the knight perished and the idea of chivalry transformed into the ideal of a righteous "An officer and gentlemen".

The symbols of chivalry are powerful, powerful because of their deep attachment to the most important virtues of man: courtesy, respect, generosity, honesty, humility, justice, excellence, courage, loyalty, duty, and defense of all women. These things are timeless.

Today, morality and ethics may seem to be in rare supply. Men no longer are taught morality; and religion is able to reach only a few, and families are often broken or like in my case, there was no one to teach me. I see the results of this disjointedness nightly on the television news, and desire for a better world.

An important thing to notice about chivalry is that the particulars of its meaning evolve. Chivalry has never stood still; that is the great reason that it is so elusive, and continues to have such power. I make it a part of my daily life, yet I don't completely understand its meaning and how it has benefited and strengthened my relationship. What I do know is it works.

IS CHIVALRY DEAD?

It might surprise you that a generation reared with a bare minimum of discipline should care about a rigorous system of morals and manners. In particular, I may wonder that men would think much of an ethic that encouraged both sexual restraint and the service of men on behalf of women. Yet I realize that today's men are hardly charmed with either the sexual revolution or the feminists' struggles to create a genderless world. I have a deeper longing for a world in which virtuous men both respect and protect women. Here is a response by some college men and woman of today, "The system of manners known as chivalry was necessary in the Middle Ages but is irrelevant today."

Chivalry indeed seemed to become irrelevant today, and what a tragic loss for both men and women. Most women refuse to hold us to the standards necessary to achieve the refined honor that has been lost. Women are disrespected everyday in today's society, because they ask for nothing more. There is probably not a woman alive who, in some part of her heart, would not want to be carried off on horseback by a knight in shining armor, but they are not allowed to admit that anymore. They are taught to declare themselves equal to men in all respects and in no need of superior treatment. If only women would realize that chivalry was a way of showing respect and devotion, we would have hope of regaining this lost system of virtue. I have come to understand that by showing respect I have gained self respect. Chivalry has provided me with virtues that allow me to be more available to women I meet, and they have come to respect me for that.

How can we bring men to this conclusion and give them the courage to act upon it? For our deliverance from a vulgarized sexuality on the one hand, and a forced old-fashioned times on the other, will begin only when men begin to contemplate the creation of a new chivalry. In other words, men must begin again to act like men, and some standards of decency must govern our relationships.

People initial response to the question of whether chivalry is dead will mostly be concern whether men still open doors for women and whether they should. This discussion can be an enormous starting point for you to come to some understanding of what your significant other values. I have found that the majority of women actually appreciate these remnants of chivalry. Most women, with one or two exceptions in every group, long for the days when men "acted like gentlemen". This was a good starting point for me to incorporate chivalry into my everyday life and to expand on it from there. Many men are under the impression that women resent having doors opened for them. This is far from the truth.

Chivalry still retains a significant place in the modern world; here are a few conduct of modern chivalry for you to follow.

CONDUCT OF MODERN CHIVALRY

1. Administer justice.
2. Always keep one's word of honor.
3. Always maintain one's principles.
4. Avoid cheating.
5. Avoid deception.
6. Avoid lying to your fellow man or woman.
7. Be polite and attentive.
8. Be respectful and honorable of women.
9. Defend the weak and innocent.
10. Die with Honor.
11. Die with valor.
12. Exhibit courage in word and deed.
13. Exhibit manners.
14. Exhibit self-control.
15. Fight for your ideals, country, and chivalry.
16. Fight with honor.
17. Live for freedom, justice and all that is good.
18. Live one's life so that it is worthy of respect and honor.

19. Loyalty to GOD, family, honor freedom and the code of chivalry.
20. Loyalty to one's friends and those who lay their trust in you.
21. Never abandon a friend, ally, or noble cause.
22. Never betray a friend.
23. Obey the law, country, and chivalry.
24. Protect the innocent.
25. Respect life and freedom.
26. Respect those of the opposite sex.
27. Show respect to authority.

I sometimes go through life oblivious to the valuable gifts that are given to me every day. A few months ago, I read a phrase which made me realize the importance of recognizing acts of kindness and chivalry.

"Men, honor all ladies. Ladies, be worthy of all honor."

There are two sides to the coin of honor and chivalry. A woman can also show chivalry, and anyone (man or woman) can appreciate a demonstration of respect.

Nothing has angered me more than when a man opens the door for a woman with her arms full and he is rebuffed by someone's twisted interpretation of women's liberation with a comment like "I could have done it myself." That woman was not acting in a manner which is worthy of honor.

We must not only exhibit chivalry and honor in our daily lives, but also graciously accept and appreciate acts of kindness, courtesy and chivalry when they are offered to us. Of course, nobody with a realistic outlook would deny that there are places in the world where discrimination and inequality still exist, but by and large, today we have an unprecedented level of opportunity and responsibility.

We have the opportunity to behave with courage, justice, mercy, generosity, faith, nobility and hope—on the job, at home, in relationships, in family matters, in our careers and in our recreational activities. By doing this, we have the opportunity to enrich our relationships, ourselves and inspire those around us.

In a tribute to the level of liberty women enjoy, and the level of equality they continue to work toward, they to have the responsibility to hold themselves to the high standards of chivalry today, rather than cutting corners or benefiting from unfair advantages and thinking people will look the other way because "she's only a woman."

Chivalry is a worthy cause, and from its very outset, women have played an important role in it. I hope that, as the understanding of chivalry today spreads and grows, there are plenty of men out there who will choose to be knights in shining armor in the 21st Century.

CHIVALRY IS NOT DEAD

FIVE WAYS TO CHOOSE GENEROSITY IN YOUR LIFE:

1. Give someone a gift, just because.
2. Don't brag about what you give.
3. Never expect anything in return for your generosity.
4. If you think someone could use some help, offer before they ask.
5. Each morning, ask yourself how you can serve humanity—then do so.

"Don't be afraid that your life will end, be afraid that it will never begin."

II

 HE KNIGHTS OF MODERN TIME

KNIGHT-HOOD

1. Champion of a cause: a fervent supporter or defender of a cause or belief.
2. Protector of a woman: a man who is protective of and devoted to a woman.
   Encarta ® World English Dictionary © & (P) 1998– 2004 Microsoft Corporation. All rights reserved.

First, there is the basic question of knighthood itself. What is it? There are general articles that speak on this point, but what does it mean today?

Knighthood exists in two places simultaneously . . . in the world and our imagination. We can speak of ideals versus realities, possibly the central problem with knighthood and the chivalric ideals. We will examine these questions from two perspectives pertaining to knightly conduct during the Middle Ages and in the romance that described their ideals. Both are important to the idea of knighthood and men today. The responsibilities of a knight are threefold. They are duty, honor, and chivalry.

Duty–A knight's first responsibilities is the welfare of the land and his family he is sworn to defend. A knight must be willing to sacrifice personal pride and will-being, as the ruler is the living symbol of the land it must be obeyed and supported in so doing, as it will not damage the land itself. A knight should be the last to complain.

Honor–A knight's second responsibility is one owed to himself more than to any other. It is to be honorable in all things, in every aspect of interaction. Honor is a concept that can not be caged in works. It is found in the heart. Knighthood is not a title of honor and privilege. Knighthood does not mean you are a master of fighting, art, or politics. Knighthood is an admission that one is human and subject to failure. It is a pledge to improve one's character and to help any who would make that journey with you. *We can only improve ourselves by enriching the lives of others.*

Lastly, what does knighthood means as it relates to the modern day?

Knighthood is not brought about by birth or wealth or by most other measures of material status. Historically, knighthood was about more than just fighting, it was also about chivalry. It is a brotherhood of virtues. Knights' were expected to be brave and honorable, to uphold the honor of women, and to protect the weak.

Chivalry is a concept that is largely ignored.

It doesn't seem to have place in the world of business, politics, relationships or personal conduct in the modern world. Women have been taught that displays of chivalry is demeaning and condescending, and men have come to believe that courtesy and respectful attitudes aren't "manly".

However, those ideas have begun to change. Current events and front-page headlines have made us all aware of the importance of ethical conduct and personal integrity. In the wake of terrorist attacks, hurricane, corporate scandals and betrayals of public trust, I and others are recognizing that duty; heroism, honesty and self-respect are more valuable today than ever before.

Men are realizing that the 21st Century needs a Code of Chivalry. I challenge men to consider how the Code of Chivalry and its Seven Knightly Virtues can be put to use in their lives each day. I want to demonstrate that chivalry can help us instill values in our children, that it can change the way we manage others and do business, which it can help establish goals and overcome challenges, that it provides a strong and unshakable means to improve our relationships.

When I've talked with women on the subject of chivalry. No matter what else someone of the group may know about chivalry, there are three words at the forefront of everyone's mind: Chivalry is dead.

Far from being dead, chivalry today is embodied by men whose actions are trustworthy and admirable; who understand that *strength and gentleness are not opposites;* and who know the importance of standing by one's principles, no matter how tempting the compromise.

Chivalry is coming more alive today than ever. I have been reevaluating the things that are important in my life, and I have discovered the virtues that the code of chivalry stands for–hope, kindness, respect, integrity and courage. I am discovering that I can still be inspired by a hero, and, best of all, I am realizing that when chivalry and equality stand side-by-side, anybody can be a knight in shining armor.

Is chivalry an idealistic goal? Without a doubt– but ideals are what sparks the imagination and fuel the soul. The ideals of chivalry eventually transformed a society of thuggish warriors into a culture of courage, respect and grace which we still think of today when we hear the term a "knight in shining armor".

In the 21st Century there is plenty of despair and darkness to be found in the neighborhoods around us. And, just like the Middle Ages, there are men today who claim that knighthood and chivalry is a thing only for children's fairy tales and scholars' doctoral. There are men who think that corporate profits and winning touchdowns and celebrity interviews are more meaningful than virtue, honor or courtesy. But hope, light and inspiration live on unstained, even after hundreds of years and no small amount of abuse. Chivalry has inspired writers, artists, police officers, fire fighters, teachers, philosophers and many others throughout the ages, not because it is mysterious and unattainable, but because it is dynamic and practical. Chivalry is far too powerful to be confined to the lecture halls.

There was no such thing as a "uniform" code of chivalry in the Middle Ages. Many people—from successful knights to philosophers—compiled lists of virtuous qualities, called the "knightly virtues," which they felt defined chivalry. No two were exactly the same. There were, however, several common themes found in these lists of knightly virtues. By combining these, here is what is considered to be *The Seven Knightly Virtues* of the modern code of chivalry:

COURAGE

More than bravado or bluster, today's knight in shining armor must have the courage of the heart necessary to undertake tasks which are difficult, tedious or unglamorous, and to graciously accept the sacrifices involved.

JUSTICE

A knight in shining armor holds himself to the highest standard of behavior, and knows that "fudging" on the little rules weakens the fabric of society for everyone.

MERCY

Words and attitudes can be painful weapons in the modern world, which is why a knight in shining armor exercises mercy in his dealings with others, creating a sense of peace and community, rather than engendering hostility and antagonism.

GENEROSITY

Sharing what's valuable in life means not just giving away material goods, but also time, attention, wisdom, and energy—the things that create a strong, rich and diverse community.

FAITH

In the code of chivalry, "faith" means trust and integrity, and a knight in shining armor is always faithful to his promises, no matter how big or small they may be.

NOBILITY

Although this word is sometimes confused with "entitlement" or "snobbishness," in the code of chivalry it conveys the importance of upholding one's convictions at all times, especially when no one else is watching.

HOPE

More than just a safety net in times of tragedy, hope is present every day in a modern knight's positive outlook and cheerful demeanor—the shining armor that shields him, and inspires people all around.

Each of these concepts is important in itself, and every one of these virtues is an admirable quality, but when all of them blend together in one person, we discover the value, and power of chivalry today. We as men today should strive to keep these virtues alive in our own hearts, but, perhaps more importantly, we should work to bring these wonderful qualities out in our relationship, people we see every day—at home, in the office, at school and on the street corner. A person who lives by the code of chivalry in today's world allows everyone to see their best qualities reflected in his shining armor.

In recent years there has been a revival of the whole fantasy about knights and the honorable lives they lived so many years ago. Consider the movie "*Braveheart.*" Mel Gibson is apparently a person who holds dearly to freedom.

Some may say men today are not looked upon as examples of what young men or boys should be. They may believe that society is falling apart because of a man's failure to be a role model, as a father and Christian.

I do not share this belief. There are men who are laying down their lives for their family, country and belief. They instilled values, virtues and chivalry in all that they do.

"Many people's reality is determined by someone else's opinion, point of view and rules."

III

OMANCE

1. Spirit of adventure: a spirit or feeling of adventure, excitement, the potential for heroic achievement, and the exotic romance of cruising down the Nile.
2. Literature medieval adventure story: a story of the adventures of chivalrous heroes written in verse or prose in a vernacular language in the Middle Ages. *Encarta ® World English Dictionary © & (P) 1998– 2004 Microsoft Corporation. All rights reserved.*

There are many of us striving for the Lancelot and the enduring life of romance. The question is how do we achieve the romance we long for?

Out of the Courtly Love movement come tales of romance, from which the legends of King Arthur arose. The symbols that have grown out of these legends are familiar to every young Westerner, King Arthur and The Knights of the Round Table, and not least, chivalry. Chivalric virtues were a crystal clear refinement of what it meant to be a fine human being, a person in search of justice and humility. The symbols of chivalry are powerful because of their deep attachment to most important virtues of man. Courtesy, respect, generosity, honesty, loyalty, humility, justice, excellence, courage and duty. These things are timeless.

Romance is powerful and should not be denied. The striving for romantic ethic has a powerful role in our world today. In the Middle Ages men and women within a certain class threw themselves at an ideal in ways rarely seen today. They called this ideal "chivalry" and held it separate from what was performed in the face of reality. A romantic ethic such as chivalry is given by poetry an enduring life, from its rough beginnings. Through its long life, such a poetic ideal not only guides and informs its reactors, but it shapes and changes itself through the actions of those who pursue it. Through whatever changes occur, the core of what I call the romance of chivalry such as loyalty, generosity, bearing, courtesy, is not in rare supply today.

THE ART OF COURTLY LOVE

- Don't use marriage as an excuse for not loving.
- He who is jealous cannot love.
- No one can be bound by a double love.
- It is well known that love is always increasing or decreasing.
- That which a lover takes against the will of his beloved has no enjoyment.
- Boys do not love until they reach the age of maturity.
- No one should be deprived of love without the very best of reasons.

- No one can love unless he is propelled by the influence of love.
- Love is always a stranger in the home of greed.
- It is not proper to love any woman who one would be ashamed to seek to marry.
- A true lover does not desire to embrace in love anyone except his beloved.
- When made public, love rarely endures.
- The easy accomplishment of love makes it of little value: difficulty of accomplishment makes it appreciated.
- Every lover regularly turns pale in the presence of this beloved.
- When a lover suddenly catches sight of his beloved his heart skips.
- A new love puts an old one to flight.
- Good character alone makes any man worthy of love.
- If love diminishes, it quickly fails and rarely revives.
- A man in love is always increasing the feeling of love.
- Jealousy increases when one suspects his beloved.
- Every act of a lover ends in the thought of his beloved.
- A true lover considers nothing good except what he thinks will please his beloved.
- A slight presumption causes a lover to suspect his beloved.
- A man who is irritated by too much passion/attention usually does not love.

SIMPLE LOVE IDEAS:

Romance does not have to be complicated. Adding that extra sparkle not only makes your partner feel special, and yourself by knowing you have made them happy, but it can also help boost your sex life in numerous ways.

LESSON #1 SMILE

You must smile. You probably think you smile now, but you don't, really. You should practice your smile in the mirror–to be big enough to be noticed, your smile will probably have to be bigger than you are used to.

LESSON #2 GET CAUGHT LOOKING

Most people look away when the object of their desire looks at them. If you want to let that person know you are interested, when she catches you looking, smile, hold eye contact a moment longer, and then look away.

LESSON #3 WAVE

A little wave to someone who caught you looking, along with a smile, is a non-intrusive, very flirty way to say "hello."

LESSON #4 WINK

You can wink at someone from across the room, or wink at someone during a conversation. If she says something funny, or someone else does something silly, you can give a wink as a way of sharing a little moment for just the two of you, as if the two of you are in on some private joke no one else is aware of.

LESSON #5 INQUIRE

You can ask "what's the story behind that? About any special or unusual thing your quarry is wearing or carrying. Examples: "that's really neat bracelet you are wearing. What's the story behind that?" or "that's a rally great briefcase. What's the story behind that?" Even if there isn't much of one, it's given you some conversation.

LESSON #6 CONNECT

While you are conversing with her, you want to be sure to have eye contact at least some of the time. At least once it's a good idea to hold the eye contact a little "too long," just a fraction too long, so there's a brief, more intimate moment between you.

LESSON #7 TOUCH

This can be as simple as placing your hand lightly on her hand for a moment, or touching her back for a moment as you walk to a table to sit down. Just do this a couple of times on the first flirting interaction–if she pulls away, don't do it again.

LESSON #8 CHECKING HER OUT

Checking out her body must be done properly. The goal is for your new friend to feel complimented that you noticed her body, not objectified like some piece of meat. You do this by making eye contact, then quickly, in less than a second, passing your eyes down and then up over her body, then back to looking in the eyes. It should happen quickly, and you should be unashamed of taking a glance. Just don't do it too often.

LESSON #9 USING THE "GOOD-BYE COMPLIMENT."

If you are shy, flirting with the "good-bye compliment" may be just the thing you need. On your way out, you simply go up to the woman you want to flirt with, and say something like, "Hi, I have to go now, but before I do, I really want to let you know that you have a really great sense of style, and that I noticed it. I wish I had more time to spend with you, but I have to go." Then leave. This allows you to build your confidence in approaching women, without having to take the risk of rejection–after all, you have to leave, you couldn't stay even if they wanted you to! (Some men ask for phone number at this point.)

CHIVALRY Is Not Dead

LESSON #10 FLIRTING

Remember, flirting should be fun, and you should leave the flirting interaction feeling victorious. Most men leave their flirting interactions feeling like failures because they don't stop until it stops being fun. If you stop flirting on a high point, while it's still fun, your new friend will feel good when thinking of you, and want to see you again.

50 THINGS YOU CAN DO FOR YOUR SIGNIFICANT OTHER.

1. Love yourself before you love anyone else.
2. Watch the sunset together.
3. Hold her w/ hands inside the back of her shirt.
4. Whisper to each other.
5. Cook for each other.
6. Make out in the rain.
7. Undress each other.
8. Hold hands.
9. Sleep together. (Actually sleep with each other-not sex)
10. Give random gifts of flowers/candy/poetry etc.
11. Roses.
12. Find out their favorite cologne/perfume and wear it every time you're together.
13. Allow her to wear your clothes.
14. Incense/candles/oils/black-lights and music make for great cuddling/sex.

15. Go for a long walk down the beach at midnight.
16. Write poetry for each other.
17. Kiss/smell her hair.
18. Hugs are the universal medicine.
19. Say I love you, only when you mean it and make sure they know you mean it.
20. Tell her that she's the only girl you ever want. Don't lie.
21. Look into each other's eyes.
22. Talk to each other using only body language and your eyes.
23. When in public, only flirt w/ each other.
24. Walk behind her and put your hands in her front pockets.
25. Put love notes in their pockets when they aren't looking.
26. Sing to each other.
27. Read to each other.
28. Public Display of Affection.
29. Take advantage of any time alone together.
30. Draw. (even if you can't).
31. Let her sit on your lap.
32. Go hiking and camp out together in the woods or on a mountain.
33. Kiss her stomach.
34. Hold her hand, stare into her eyes, kiss her hand and then put it over your heart.
35. Unless you can feel their heart beating, you aren't close enough.
36. Dance together.

37. I love the way a girl looks right after she's fallen asleep with her heading my lap.
38. Carry her to bed.
39. Brush her hair out of her face for her.
40. Act out mutual fantasies together. (Not necessarily sexual)
41. Never forget the kiss goodnight. And always remember to say, "Sweet dreams."
42. Go to church/pray/worship together.
43. Make sacrifices for each other.
44. Even if you are really busy doing something, go out of your way to call and say I love you.
45. Remember your dreams and tell her about them.
46. Be Prince Charming to her parents. (brownie points)
47. Hang out with his/her friends. (more brownie points)
48. Take her to see a romantic movie and remember the parts she liked.
49. Make sacrifices for each other.
50. Hold her around her hips/sides.

20 IDEAS TEENAGERS IN LOVE

1. Go to church/pray/worship together.
2. Love yourself before you love anyone else.
3. Make excuses for calling them every 5 minutes.
4. Ever if you are really busy doing something, go out of your way to call and say I love you.
5. Remember your dreams and tell her about them.
6. Ride your bike 8 miles just to see them for a few hours.

7. Ride home and call them. Tell her your most sacred secrets/fears.
8. Be prince Charming to her parents. (brownie points).
9. Hang out with her friends (more brownie points).
10. Take her to see romantic movie and remember the parts she liked.
11. Learn from each other and don't make the same mistake twice.
12. Everyone deserves a second chance.
13. Make sacrifices for each other.
14. Really love each other, or don't stay together.
15. Stand up for them when someone talks trash.
16. Watch the sunset together.
17. Write poetry for each other.
18. Tell her that she doesn't have to do anything she doesn't want to. And mean it.
19. Sing to each other.
20. Read to each other.

"No man behaves as a complete gentleman all the time, but the best men never cease yearning to."

IV

CHANGE

1. Change: alter, modify, convert, vary, shift, transform, transmute
2. Core meaning: to make or become different; change the most general term; alter a narrow term, often suggesting a change in an aspect of something rather than in its entirety; modify to make minor changes or alterations, especially in order to improve something.

Encarta ® World English Dictionary © & (P) 1998–2004 Microsoft Corporation. All rights reserved.

Change is unavoidable. When change is embraced it is joyful, when you don't embrace change, it will come anyway, and drags you along painfully. This is why I was in pain; because I had not embraced the power of change.

I didn't like change and in fact I was not aware of change happening in my life. But, change must occur; the secret is I have the power to determine the outcome of change. When I am not conscious of change, it dragged me along and that is unconscious living, to be dragged along not knowing what for and where I was going. It had occur to me before I end my day to ask myself, what did I do today? What have I achieved? I become conscious of how my day really took place.

Change means growth or aging, I can choose which one. There are many of us that have not grown but have aged with time. To grow is to increase mentally, physically, and emotionally. The ability to grow is to do more with less energy. When I was not in synch with change, change made me age and age is to wither or fade away. When I was a teenager, I was eager to let everyone know I'm a teenager and I would even shout "I'm thirteen". I wanted to grow up so much; I was in synch with change. Over time I stopped growing; when did I stop growing physically, mentally, emotionally, and spiritually? I stopped growing when I fell out of synch with change. When people turn 40 or 50 years old they would tell people that "age is just a number". What is the deepest reason why they can't say their age? Is it because there is some fear in their conscious mind that they have accepted that growing old means limitation, weakness, diseases, and all the negative things. Growing older should not mean weakness or limitations, growing older means you are respected, knowledgeable, you are loved by many and everyone comes to you. You can pretend in your actions, but you can not pretend in your thinking. Your unconscious mind knows the truth. Just as you are saying, "Oh, age is nothing but a number," deep within there is fear, and the thing you fear your mind can attract.

CHIVALRY Is Not Dead

*"The only thing we can count on is change.
Why not welcome it."*

We must all die, but we don't have to go through life in pain. The way to move forward is to know change and be in synch with change and determine what your life will be. Life is hard and you are afraid to move forward. That is because you have not mastered change. Change must occur and a simple practice for you is to take power over change. You must ask yourself moment by moment, what was I like yesterday? What was I today, and what is different?

Being conscious of change, you partake in the magic of your own life unfolding; you are a mystery coming into yourself. When you allow your spirit to guide you, you will be rejuvenated.

Often people think changing your mind means you are a weak being. That is not true; the truth is your mind changes moment to moment. The thing you should ask yourself is what am I changing my mind from and what am I changing it to?

The unconscious being does not know what he is changing from or too. Conscious living is for you to ask yourself, what am I thinking and what am I changing my mind to and why am I changing it to this? That is conscious living, and it places you in the power of change; change must not change the spiritual being. Change will occur, but you are created in the spirit and likeness of GOD, you have the power to move change, halt change, and redirect change to take charge over your life. Over time change will seek your permission before it does anything in your life. The goal to be in a spiritual place where change will pause, wait and ask your permission. That is your power you had it in the beginning and you can have it again.

The answer to what we shall be is contained in what we are now thinking. For you can change your thinking!

Earnest Holmes

You're going to change the world today.

No, don't try to deny it. And you know I understand that it can be a little overwhelming, to have the entire world depending on you, but I know that you can do it.

Actually, I knew you could do it when I first met you. When I first saw the hunger in your fingertips and the fire in your eyes.

When you spoke in just that way, with just those words, in just that rhythm that said, "I'm going to change the world. Gonna make it a little better, a little sweeter, a bit more true."

And I remember the way you said that nothing on this or any other planet was going to stop you. Then you turned and walked away, confident and clear.

And I remember thinking to me that you were amazing, that I'd never met anyone quite like you, and I was sure that, if you put your mind and hands to it, there were nothing that could break you.

So there you sit, knowing that today's the day. Because I see the way you're shifting nervously in your chair, the way your body crackles and zaps, the way your grin says that you've decided that there is no time like now to move.

You're going to change the world today.

I'm just glad I was here to see it.

Strong lives are motivated by dynamic purpose.

Kenneth Hildebrand

V

MASLOW'S HIERARCHY OF NEEDS

Maslow was one of the key figures that changed a prevailing atmosphere of subconscious demons and heavy emphasis on psychological measurement. The more enlightened deeper side of man was put aside. It was just not scientific or helpful to the people with sick brains. (Or at least so they thought.)

Both the B-Values and Hierarchy of Needs were in sharp contrast to the simple mechanics of behaviorism introduced by Watson in 1919 and later by Skinner. Behaviorism was strictly observational and based solely on measurements. "If you don't see it, don't think about it" was the premise. Behaviorism was soulless and based merely on stimuli and reinforcement. Behaviorism was one of many schools of psychology that debased man. For example, psychoanalysis taught that man was ruled by an unconscious mind and energized solely by animal instincts.

Maslow's introduction of B-Values and related

concepts changed psychology forever. Maslow elevated psychology to study a deeper and more complex man. Instead of sick man study, Maslow did great man study. In studied the greatest people in history and cataloged what they had in common that made them great.

Maslow drew his famous Hierarchy of Needs Pyramid in the late 1960s. This pyramid is shown in the figure below, except I added the yellow Spiritual layer.

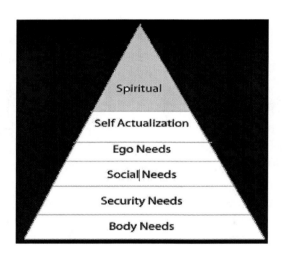

MASLOW LAYERS ARE DEFINED AS:

Body (Physiological) Needs such as air, warmth, food, sleep, stimulation and activity. The Body needs are biological. These needs can be very strong because if deprived over time, the person will die.

Security (Safety) Needs such as living in a safe area away from threats. This level is more likely to be found in children as they have a greater need to feel safe

Social (Love and Belongingness) Needs such as the love of family and friends

Ego (Self esteem) Needs such as healthy pride The Ego needs focus on our need for self-respect, and respect from others.

Self Actualization (Fulfillment) Needs such as purpose, personal growth and realization of potentials. The point where people become fully functional, acting purely on their own volition and having a healthy personality. The Self-Actualization is described by Maslow as an ongoing process involved in a cause outside their skin. People on this level work at something very precious, call it a vocation or calling in the old priestly sense. These people are very fine, healthy, strong, sagacious (very smart) and creative. Maslow included saintly people on this level.

I have extended the needs to include one more need. Beyond Self Actualization are the **Spiritual Needs**. What is unique about the Spiritual Needs is that one can jump to the spiritual needs from any level of need. A person can attune to GOD and spiritual love when everything else is going bad. If we consider each of the needs to be associated with its corresponding state of consciousness, then there is a state of grace when one is guided with deep purpose and divine directions.

Maslow's Hierarchy of Needs is a simplification, but it is of great historical importance. Maslow was one of the first in his field to study above normal people.

To me self actualization is freedom . . . But going a step further in the spiritual world, not only brings freedom, but a deep and lasting peace. It is like the rest of the mind becomes in alignment and is balanced. The power of course comes from the Spiritual world, where we receive guidance.

GETTING BACK TO SELF ACTUALIZATION AND ITS FREEDOM WE FIND:

- Wholeness, unity integration, and oneness -this is part of the spiritual   experience.
- Perfection, just rightness - this is taught in classes in spirituality.
- Completion, ending, destiny, fate -fate is not taught in classes on spirituality.
- Justice, search for truth, orderliness, this is part of spirituality.
- Simplicity, beauty, goodness, uniqueness, effortlessness, playfulness, truth, self sufficiency -again this part of spirituality.

WITHIN THE PEACE AND DEPTH WE FIND THAT WE BECOME DRIVEN WITH NEW NEEDS:

- Need to feel close to GOD
- Need to Pray
- Need to Meditate
- Need of Purity

There is One Infinite Mind from which all things come . . . Consequently, the Infinite is in and through man and is in and though everything. Act as though I am and I will be.

VI

WHAT ARE YOU COMMITTED TO?

One of the secrets to a fulfilling life is to daily recognize exactly where my commitments lie. I speak not of appointments, but to principles, to the guiding purpose of my life. My primary commitment to GOD. To be it and see it as the most important things in my life, day in and day out. I'm committed to taking good care of myself, but sometimes I forget and have to be reminded, never chastised, instead gently but firmly reminded.

Sometimes I let my commitment to myself be forgotten in my commitment to being loving with others. I notice that I suffer from feeling that others don't keep their commitments. They haven't made a commitment to themselves and their world is reflecting that. I spoke with a credit manager who said that if his boss asked him to do something that he felt was unkind to a client he'd have to do it because that was his job. His commitment was to the boss, rather than kindness. How many times a day do we see that kind of choice in people' commitments play out in our lives?

Sometimes people are committed to being kind and loving with others, but not themselves. In a world where there are so many wonderful things to do I want to commit to doing less of them so that I have more time to just be wonderful unto myself and my loved ones. I find it a challenging commitment to keep and I see the price I pay for not keeping my agreements.

I need to ask myself every day, what am I really committed to? I need to keep my commitments because the quality of my life reflects the integrity of my commitments.

By Claire Pearce

VII

⚜ODES OF CHIVALRY

THE TEN COMMANDMENTS OF THE CODE OF CHIVALRY

Prowess: To seek excellence on all endeavors expected of a knight, martial and otherwise, seeking strength to be used in the service of justice, rather than in personal aggrandizement.

Justice: Seek always the path of 'right', unencumbered by his or own personal interest. Recognize that the sword of justice can be a terrible thing, so it must be tempered by humanity and mercy. If the 'right' you see rings not with others, and you seek it out without bending to the temptation for expediency, then you will earn renown beyond measure.

Truth: Speak always the truth. To lie is to dishonor you lord, yourself, and the power of Good. It is an injustice.

Loyalty: Be known for unwavering commitment to your lord and ideals you choose to live by. There are many places where compromise is expected; loyalty is not amongst them.

Defense: The ideal knight was sworn by oath to defend his liege lord and those who depended upon him. Seek always to defend your kingdom, your family, and those to whom you believe worthy of loyalty.

Courage: Being a knight often means choosing the more difficulty path, the personally expensive one. Be prepared to make personal sacrifices in service of the beliefs and people you value. At the same time, a knight should seek wisdom to see that stupidity and courage are cousins. Courage also means taking the side of truth in all matters, rather than seeking the expedient lie. Seek the truth whenever possible, but remember to temper justice with mercy, or the pure truth can bring grief.

Faith: A knight must have faith in his beliefs, for faith roots him and gives hope against the despair that human failings create.

Humility: Value first the contributions of others; do not boast of your own accomplishments, let others do this for you. Tell the deeds of others before your own, according them the renown rightfully earned though virtuous deeds. In this way the office of knighthood is well done and glorified, helping not only the

gentle spoken of but also all who call themselves knights.

Largesse: Be generous in so far as your resources allow; largesse used in this way counters gluttony. It also makes the path of mercy easier to discern when a difficult decision of justice is required.

Nobility: Seek great stature of character by holding to the virtues and duties of knight, realizing that though the ideals cannot be reached, the quality of striving towards them ennobles the spirit, growing the character from dust towards the heavens. Nobility also has the tendency to influence others, offering a compelling example of what can be done in the service of rightness.

Franchise: Seek to emulate everything I have spoken of as sincerely as possible, not for the reason of personal gain but because it is right. Do not restrict your exploration to a small idea, but seek to infuse every aspect of your life with these qualities. Should you succeed in even a tiny measure then you will be well remembered for your quality and virtue.

VIII

 HE TRUTH

In truth there was no such code; chivalry was a set of ideals and duties changed though out Middle Ages to meet new socio-economic realities. In our day, they must once again change, maintaining the essential quality of defending "rightness" by binding the main images of what we call "chivalry."

Chivalry is often taken to be a matter of opinion and disputed, but most would agree that the previous virtues all have a place in world today. There will be grave differences of opinion on what duties and actions are expected in service of these virtues, and of their relative importance to one another, but I hope this serves as a starting point of discussion.

We must be obedient to the whole of our truth . . . If we can do that the words of truth will continue to be given, and we will be given the power to live them more fully.

Parker J. Palmer

IBLIOGRAPHY

A. H. Maslow The Farther Reaches of Human Nature, Esalen Books, Viking Press
SBN 670-30853-6 hardbound, 670-00360-3 softbound

Abraham H. Maslow Toward a Psychology of Being, D. Van Nostrand Company, 1968
Library of Congress Catalog Card Number 68-30757

Abraham Maslow was an American psychologist who published in his book *Motivation and Personality* (1943) his famous Hierarchy of Needs.

George Norwood , Deepermind, www.deepermind.com

What Am I Committed to? By Jennifer Hadley, Inner Visions; A Guide for Daily Inspiration published January 2005 by Agape Int'l Spiritual Center, Culver City, CA 90230

The Art of Courtly Love by Andreas Capellanus.

1. Before you started this book, what are your thoughts and convictions about chivalry and knighthood? The reason for this is for you to get a picture of what you know about chivalry, knighthood and the importance it plays in your life.

I believe chivalry does apply to today's world.

I believe that I can change my life's course.

I believe my responsibilities are? Check those which apply.

Duty to family

Loyalty to family

Honor to self

Be polite and attentive

Defend the weak and innocent

Avoid deception

I believe that virtues have to do with me.

I believe that "encouraging" others provides strength that will enable them to face and even conquer their difficulties.

I believe that teaching others is for those in positions of leadership.

I believe that I have a responsibility for the progress of others.

I believe that my daily social interaction with others is an integral part of my responsibility for their growth and mine.

I believe in opening doors for men and woman.

I believe in defending all women.

I believe that men should take responsibility to teach other men.

I believe that I have the virtues of a knight.

I believe that I can direct change in my life.

I believe that I need to be understood.

I know that there values I need to be at my best.

I know what I am committed to.

I know I must honor my commitments because the quality of my life reflects the integrity of my commitments.

I know I must practice The Ten Commandments of the Codes of Chivalry.

I know there are chivalric things that I can do for my significant other.

I know how to be more romantic.

I know that chivalry, bravery, and honor are thought to be characteristics of a knight.

CHAPTER I

1. What does chivalry mean to you?
2. What reshaped the idea of the social warrior?
3. What new virtues were added to the ideal knight?
4. What other secular influence arose that had an equally strong say in the new knighthood?
5. How can the virtues of the ideal knight work in your life?
6. Are the virtues of knighthood a part of your life and those around you?

CHAPTER II:

1. What does knighthood mean to you?
2. What virtues do you follow today?
3. How can chivalry be apart of your life?
4. What does chivalry mean to you?
5. Is chivalry practiced in your life?
6. What virtues mean the most to you?
7. What can be done to improve the virtues of today's man?
8. In your day to day activity do you see acts of virtue?
9. How can you teach virtues to the youth around you?

CHAPTER III:

1. What does romance mean to you?
2. Is there romance in your life?
3. How can one be more romantic?

4. What do you do now romantically?
5. What are three virtues in romance?
6. Is romance a thing of the past and if so why?

2. Now that you've completed this book, what are your thoughts on chivalry and knighthood?

I now believe chivalry does apply to today's world.

I now believe that I can change my life course.

I now believe my responsibilities are? Check those which apply.

Duty to family

Loyalty to family

Honor to self

Be polite and attentive

Defend the weak and innocent

Avoid deception

I now believe that virtues have to do with me.

I now believe that "encouraging" others involves putting strength into them to   enable them to face and even conquer their difficulties.

I now believe that teaching or correcting others is for those in positions of leadership.

I now believe that I have a responsibility for the progress of others.

I now believe that my daily social interaction with others is an integral part of my responsibility for their growth and mine.

I now believe in holding open doors for men and woman alike.

I now believe in defending all women.

I now believe that men should take responsibility to teach other men.

I now believe that I have the virtues of a knight.

I now believe that I can direct change in my life.

I now believe that I do not need to be understood.

I now know that there values I need to be at my best.

I now know what I am committed to.

I now know I must keep my commitments because the quality of my life reflects the integrity of my commitments.

I now know I must practice The Ten Commandments of the Code of Chivalry.

I now know things that I can do for my significant other.

I now know how to be more romantic.

I now know that the qualities of chivalry, bravery, and honor are thought to be characteristics of a knight.

Reflect on your relationship with others, including family members. Think especially of those you have a "problem" with because of the length or depth of the connection. Have you failed to assume responsibility for anyone's growth in these relationships? If so, list them and explain how you've failed them and how you will change them.

Contact author Anthony Ray Williams
or order more copies of this book at

TATE PUBLISHING, LLC

127 East Trade Center Terrace
Mustang, Oklahoma 73064

(888) 361 - 9473

Tate Publishing, LLC

www.tatepublishing.com